English made easy

Preschool
ages 3–5
The Alphabet

Author Su Hurrell

Certificate ☆ ☆ ☆ ★

Congratulations to ....

for successfully finishing this book.

☆ *You're a star!* ☆

DK

Letter sounds: **a**

a a

Draw lines joining the sound in the middle to the pictures that **begin** with the same sound.

a

b

b b

Draw lines joining the sound in the middle to the pictures that **begin** with the same sound.

b

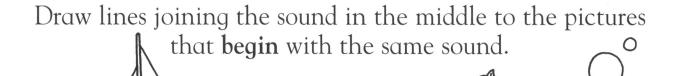

c c

Draw lines joining the sound in the middle to the pictures
that **begin** with the same sound.

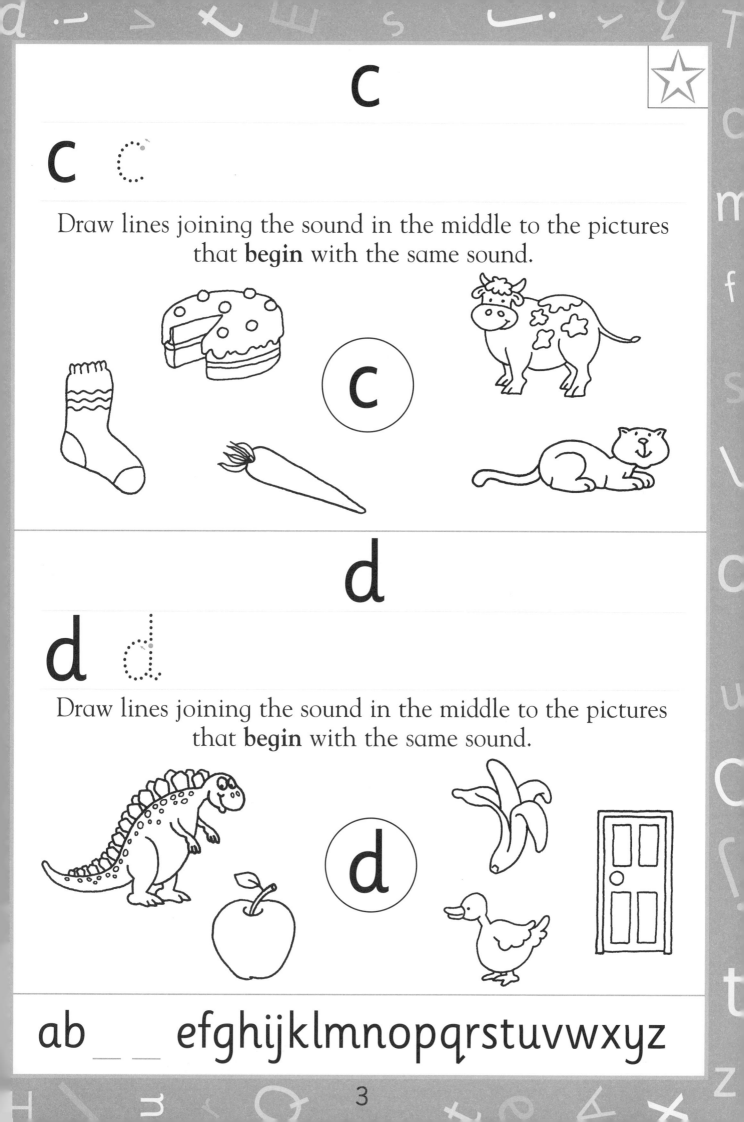

d

d d

Draw lines joining the sound in the middle to the pictures
that **begin** with the same sound.

ab ___ efghijklmnopqrstuvwxyz

e

e e

Draw lines joining the sound in the middle to the pictures that **begin** with the same sound.

f

f f

Draw lines joining the sound in the middle to the pictures that **begin** with the same sound.

abcd ___ ghijklmnopqrstuvwxyz

g

g g

Draw lines joining the sound in the middle to the pictures that **begin** with the same sound.

h

h h

Draw lines joining the sound in the middle to the pictures that **begin** with the same sound.

abcdef __ ijklmnopqrstuvwxyz

Odd one out

Look at the box in each row, then draw a (ring) around the picture that does not begin with the sound in the box.

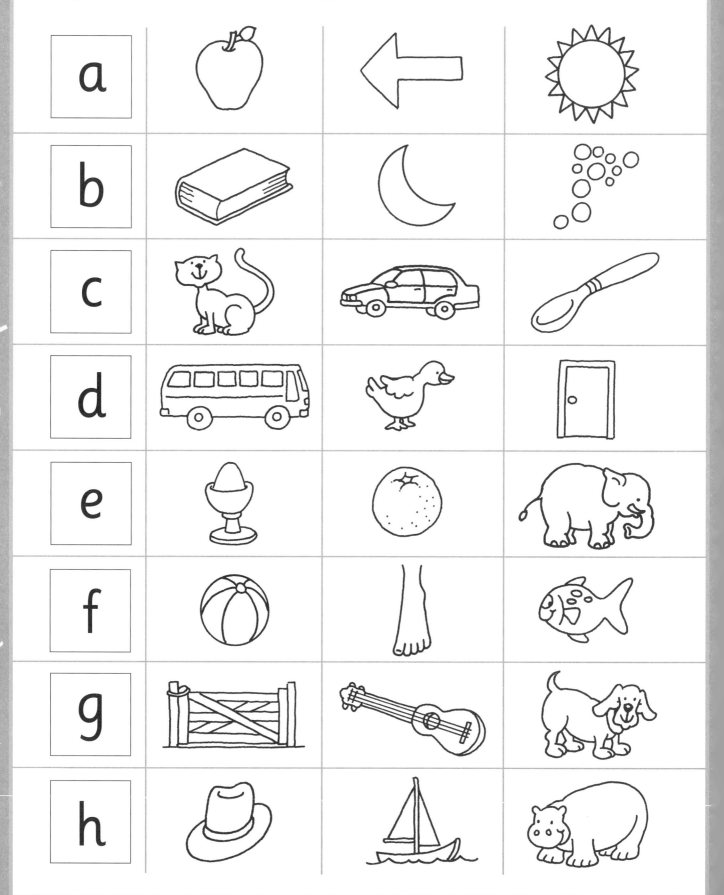

Missing letters

Fill in the missing letter in each word. As a clue, it will be one of the letters at the bottom of the page.

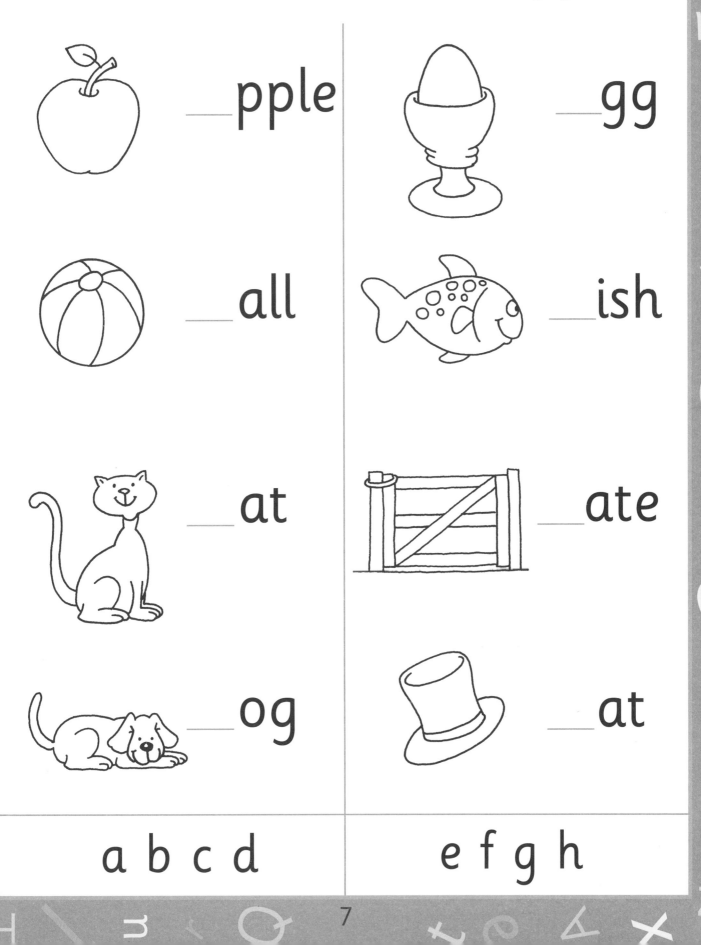

_pple

_gg

_all

_ish

_at

_ate

_og

_at

a b c d   e f g h

☆

i

i i

Draw lines joining the sound in the middle to the pictures that **begin** with the same sound.

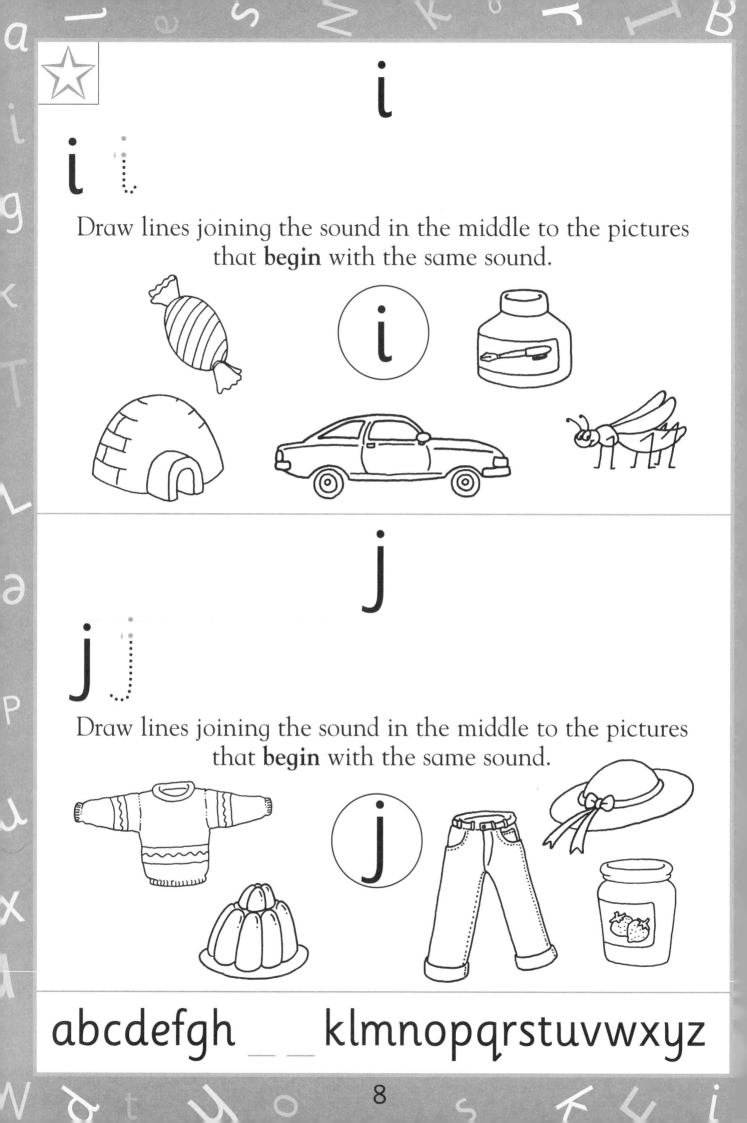

j

j j

Draw lines joining the sound in the middle to the pictures that **begin** with the same sound.

abcdefgh _ _ klmnopqrstuvwxyz

k

k k

Draw lines joining the sound in the middle to the pictures
that **begin** with the same sound.

l

l l

Draw lines joining the sound in the middle to the pictures
that **begin** with the same sound.

abcdefghij __ __ mnopqrstuvwxyz

9

m

m m

Draw lines joining the sound in the middle to the pictures that **begin** with the same sound.

n

n n

Draw lines joining the sound in the middle to the pictures that **begin** with the same sound.

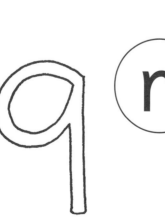

abcdefghijkl _ _ opqrstuvwxyz

o

o ⭕

Draw lines joining the sound in the middle to the pictures that **begin** with the same sound.

p

p p

Draw lines joining the sound in the middle to the pictures that **begin** with the same sound.

abcdefghijklmn __qrstuvwxyz

Odd one out

Look at the box in each row, then draw a (ring) around the picture that does not begin with the sound in the box.

Missing letters

Fill in the missing letter in each word. As a clue, it will be one of the letters at the bottom of the page.

___ewels

___agpie

___angaroo

___eedle

___ion

___alm

i j k l

m n o p

q

q q

Draw lines joining the sound in the middle to the pictures that **begin** with the same sound.

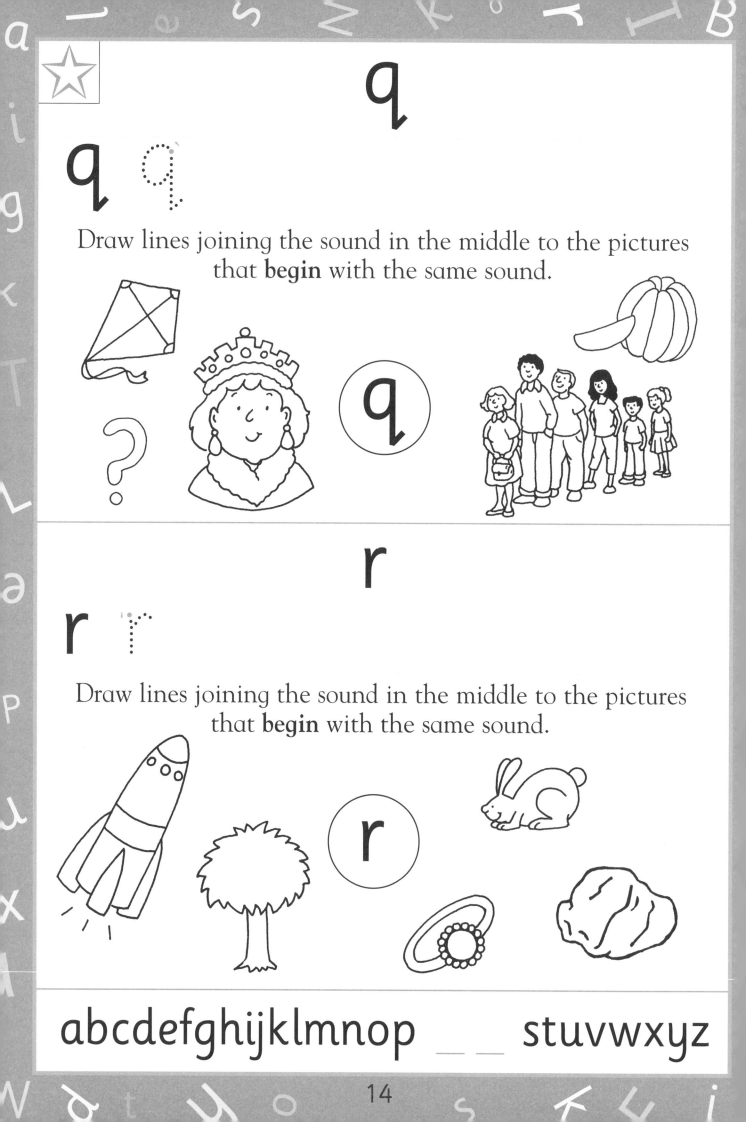

r

r r

Draw lines joining the sound in the middle to the pictures that **begin** with the same sound.

abcdefghijklmnop   stuvwxyz

s

s s

Draw lines joining the sound in the middle to the pictures that **begin** with the same sound.

s

t

t t

Draw lines joining the sound in the middle to the pictures that **begin** with the same sound.

t

abcdefghijklmnopqr __ __ uvwxyz

u

u ⠄ᴜ̈

Draw lines joining the sound in the middle to the pictures that **begin** with the same sound.

v

V ⠄v̈

Draw lines joining the sound in the middle to the pictures that **begin** with the same sound.

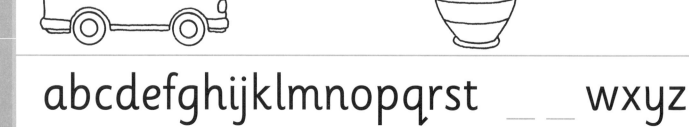

abcdefghijklmnopqrst   wxyz

W

W w

Draw lines joining the sound in the middle to the pictures that **begin** with the same sound.

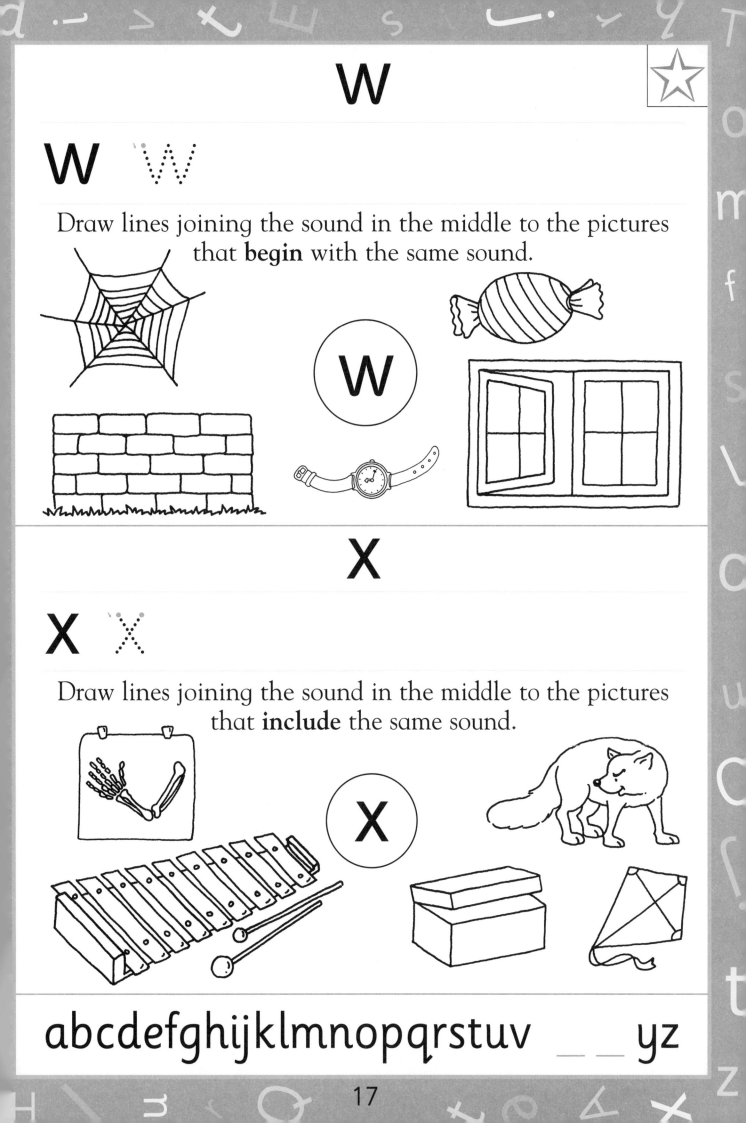

X

X x

Draw lines joining the sound in the middle to the pictures that **include** the same sound.

abcdefghijklmnopqrstuv __ __ yz

y

y y

Draw lines joining the sound in the middle to the pictures that **begin** with the same sound.

z

z z

Draw lines joining the sound in the middle to the pictures that **begin** with the same sound.

abcdefghijklmnopqrstuvwx

Odd one out

Look at the box in each row, then draw a (ring) around the picture that does not begin with the sound in the box.

Fill in the missing letter in each word.
It will be one of the letters at the bottom of the page.

_mbrella   _atch

iolin   fo

q r s t u v w x y z

19

⭐ Small letters and capitals

Draw a line joining the letters that make the same sound.

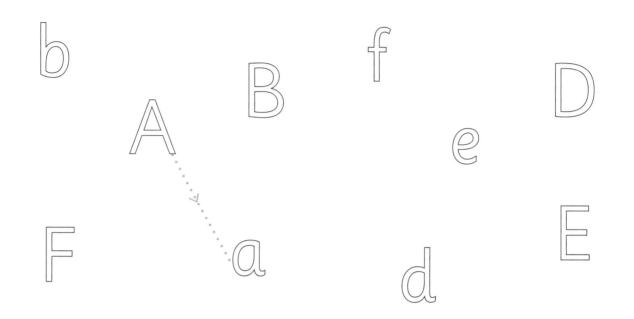

b   f   D

B

A   e

F   a   d   E

Draw a line joining the letters that make the same sound.

M   T   N

t

m   j   n

J   R   r

Draw a line joining the letters that make the same sound.

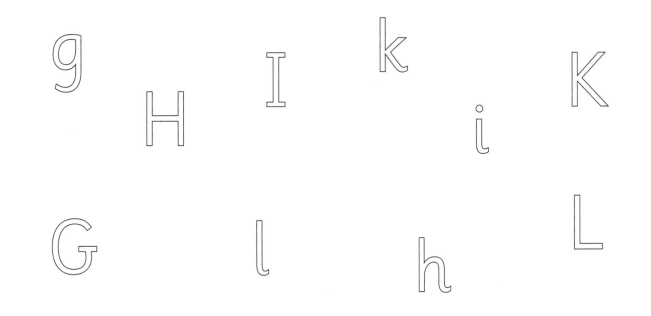

Draw a line joining the letters that make the same sound.

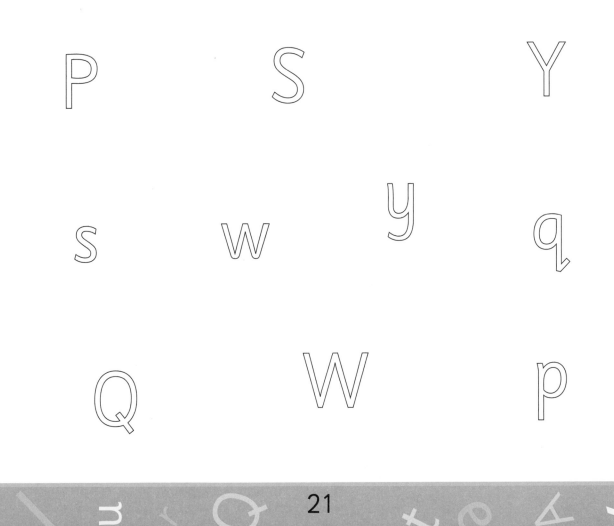

21

Vowel sounds: **a**

Draw lines joining the vowel sound **a** to the pictures that have the same sound in the **middle**.

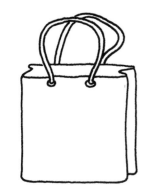
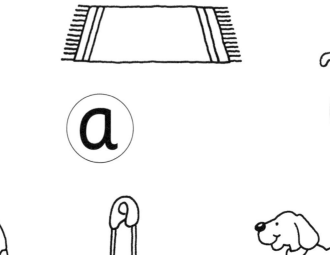

Fill in the missing letter in each word.

 c _ p   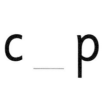 f _ n

 b _ g   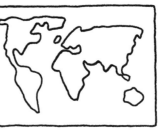 m _ p

 b _ t    h _ nd

e

Draw lines joining the vowel sound **e** to the pictures that have the same sound in the **middle**.

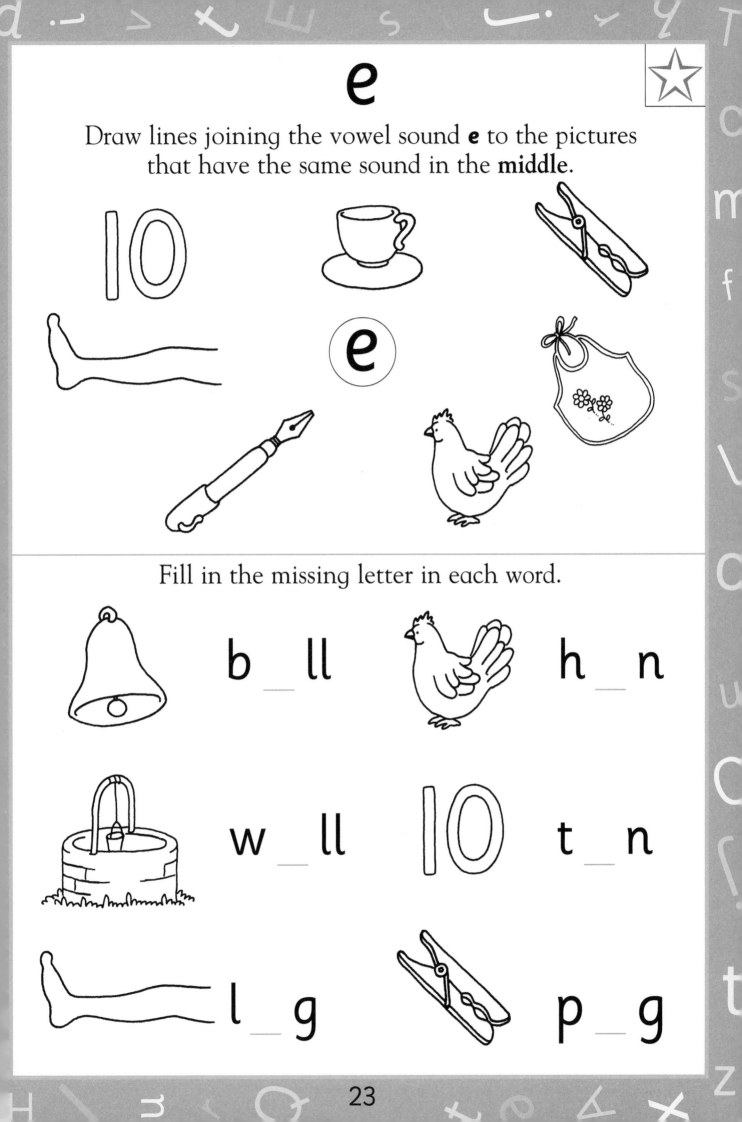

Fill in the missing letter in each word.

b _ ll

h _ n

w _ ll

t _ n

l _ g

p _ g

Draw lines joining the vowel sound **i** to the pictures that have the same sound in the **middle.**

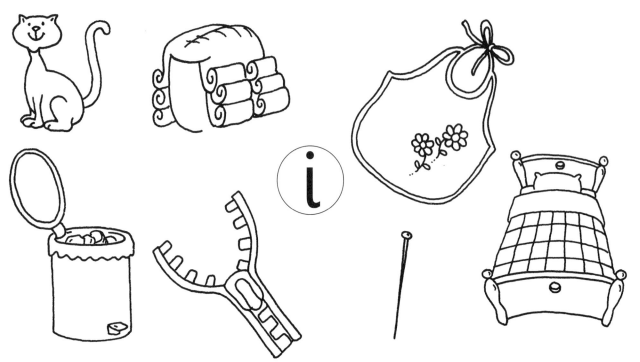

Fill in the missing letter in each word.

 h _ ll    d _ sh

 t _ n    f _ sh

p _ n    p _ g

o

Draw lines joining the vowel sound **o** to the pictures that have the same sound in the **middle**.

o

Fill in the missing letter in each word.

p _ p

s _ ck

d _ ts

f _ x

m _ p

l _ ck

25

u

Draw lines joining the vowel sound **u** to the pictures that have the same sound in the **middle**.

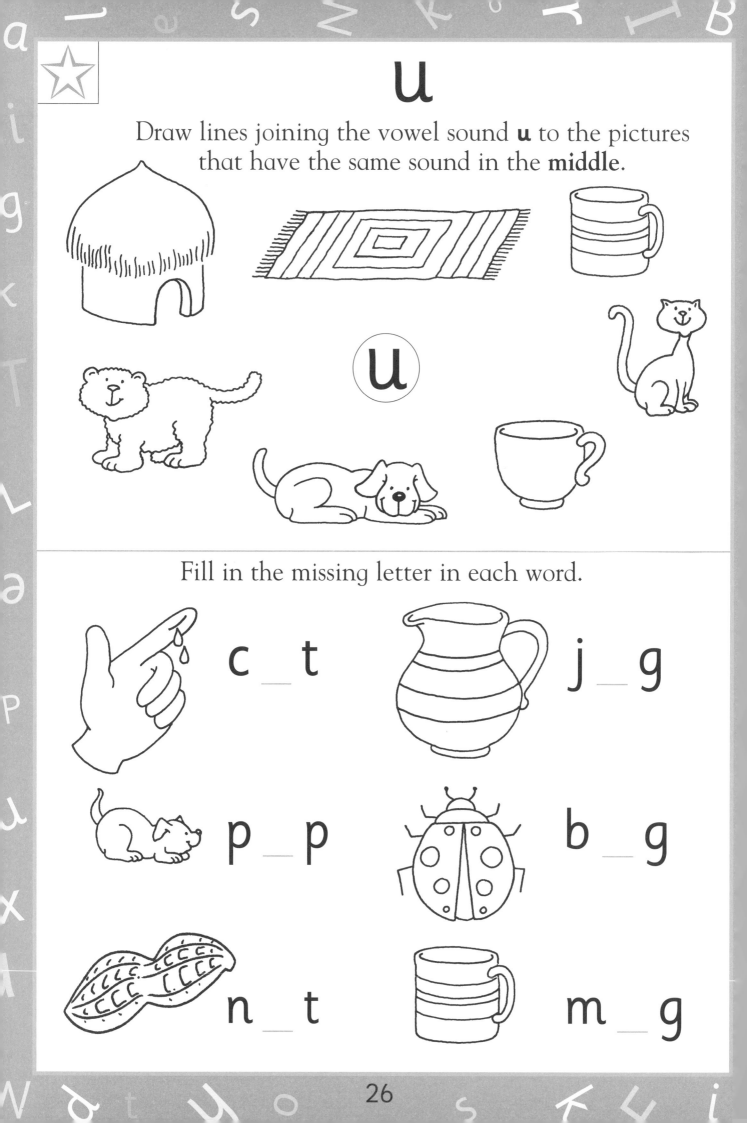

Fill in the missing letter in each word.

c _ t

j _ g

p _ p

b _ g

n _ t

m _ g

A story

Finish the story by filling in the missing letters.
The picture clues will help you.

One day the  s__n was shining. The

d__g was sleeping. The c__t was

sleeping. But the h__n saw a f__x.

"Help! Help!" she cried.

The __at and the __og

hid in a b__n. The __en flew

into a h__t. The fo__ jumped

into a b__ __ , and the __ __n

went on shining.

Puzzle page

Write the missing letters in the boxes.

Puzzle page

Write the missing letters in the boxes.

Play I spy

How many things begin with the letters at the bottom of the page? Write the number in the box beside the letter.

b

t

Play I spy

How many things begin with the letters at the bottom of the page? Write the number in the box beside the letter.

f ☐   h ☐   g ☐

Play I spy

How many things begin with the letters at the bottom of the page? Write the number in the box beside the letter.

p

w

u

l

Notes for Parents

This book is designed to help your child learn early reading skills by focusing on the different sounds of each of the letters in the alphabet. This method of teaching reading is called *phonics*. The naming, matching and writing activities will encourage your child to learn the names of each letter, as well as the different sounds each letter makes and how it is written on the page. By completing the pages of this book, your child will discover that print carries meaning and that reading and writing are both fun and interesting skills to learn.

Content

By working through this book, your child will learn:
- to write the letters of the alphabet as small letters;
- to match the small letters with their corresponding capital letters;
- to put letters in alphabetical order;
- to match the initial letters of words to letter sounds;
- to recognise the sounds of the five vowels when in the middle of words;
- to develop eye-and-hand co-ordination;
- to practise handwriting skills;
- to write from left to right on the page;
- to understand that letters go together to create words;
- to develop an awareness of simple spelling.

How to help your child with the alphabet

One fun and simple way of helping your child to memorise the names of letters and to remember alphabetical order is to sing the letters of the alphabet together. In addition to learning letter names, it is just as important that you familiarise your child with the different sounds that each letter makes.

Always pronounce the letters with short sounds. For example, say "b" and not "ber"; say "h" like a panting sound and not "her". By introducing your child to these short letter sounds, you are laying the foundations for accurate word building and spelling at a later stage. If long sounds are used, it can present difficulties when your child begins to read new words. For example, if you say the letters *c – a– t* with short sounds, it is possible to sound out the word correctly; however, if you say the same letters with long sounds, *cer – aa – ter*, your child will not be able to produce the word *cat*.

Practise letter names and sounds with your child in the course of your daily routine. However, when your child is just starting to learn letter sounds, it is important to keep the words simple and the initial letter sounds very obvious. Try to avoid words that start with letter blends (combined sounds such as *sh*, *th* and *br*). You can help make some letters more memorable if you link them to familiar things. For example, you could say that the letter *s* sounds like the hissed "sss" of a snake and also that the letter *s* looks similar to the shape of snake.

Once your child is familiar with the basic letter sounds, you can then extend his or her vocabulary and experience by introducing words with letter blends. An enjoyable way of doing this is to play a game of *I spy*.

How to use this book

Writing materials
Your child should have a pencil that is sharpened, but not too pointed. A soft lead pencil (2B) is preferable for the writing activities. If the pencil is too hard, your child's writing may be difficult to see on the page, which could lead to frustration.

As each activity involves colouring pictures, your child will need a range of colouring pencils or felt-tip pens – not the type that bleed through paper, as they will spoil subsequent pages. Avoid crayons, as these are likely to be too thick for accurately colouring the pictures and so could lead your child to become frustrated with his or her achievements.

Pencil grip
It is important to encourage your child to hold a pencil correctly. Your child should pick up the pencil in the dominant hand and hold it between the thumb and first finger. The second finger goes beneath the pencil to support it. Make sure that the pencil is not gripped too tightly and not held too close to the tip. It should rest at an angle of 45 degrees between the first finger and the thumb. If your child has problems, it can help if you make a grip for the pencil using some Plasticine. Mould a small piece into a three-sided pyramid, and push the pencil through the middle – this will encourage your child to place his or her fingers correctly.

Getting the most from the activities

Work through this book in page order. The book progresses from individual letters of the alphabet and vowel sounds to more difficult letter puzzles. It is important not to miss out any of these stages as the contents have been carefully planned to take your child through a progression of early reading and writing skills.

If your child is struggling with the activities, don't worry. He or she may not be ready for this book or may only be able to do the first few activities. If this happens, leave the book for a while, and continue to practise listening for initial letter sounds in simple words with your child. Later on, return to the book, recapping on any pages he or she may have already completed.

If your child has enjoyed a particular activity or is having some difficulty with it, try doing some additional practice on scrap paper. You may find it helpful to have some extra paper to hand before you start your activity sessions.

Working through the activities in this book should be an enjoyable shared experience for both you and your child, so choose a moment when you have time to concentrate and your child is not too tired or hungry. Read the instructions aloud, making sure that your child understands what he or she is expected to do for each activity.

Don't spend too long on each activity session – it's better to keep it short and fun and to let your child get a feel for the reading skills involved. Celebrate your child's success, and build his or her confidence by giving plenty of praise and encouragement along the way.

Page-by-page notes

Pages 2, 3, 4 and 5 – Letter sounds: a, b, c, d, e, f, g and h

These activities introduce the letters *a* to *h*. There are several exercises on each page. First, name each new letter and its sound. Then, ask your child to practise writing the letter by first tracing over the dots and then copying the letter several times. Next, say together the name of each picture out loud. Emphasise the sound at the beginning of each word. Ask your child to draw a line to link the featured letter with the pictures that begin with the same initial letter sound. Finally, complete the letters of the alphabet at the bottom of the page by filling in the missing letters. Make sure that the two letters are written in the correct order. Reinforce the letter order by saying the alphabet through each time.

pages 2 and 3

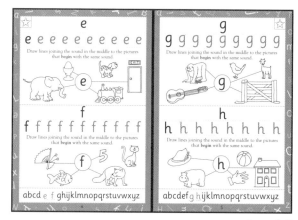

pages 4 and 5

Pages 6 and 7 – Odd one out and Missing letters

These activities provide revision exercises featuring the group of letters from the previous four pages. On page 6, ask your child to look at the letter in the box on the left. Say together the sound, and then name the pictures in the row. Your child should then draw a ring around the picture that doesn't begin with this letter sound. On page 7, words are introduced to enable your child to gain some experience of looking at how words are constructed. Say together the name of each picture. Ask your child to identify the initial letter sound and then complete the word by writing down the missing initial letter.

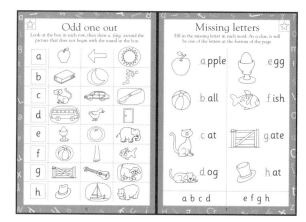

pages 6 and 7

Pages 8, 9, 10 and 11 – Letters sounds: i, j, k, l, m, n, o and p

These activities introduce the letters *i* to *p*. The exercises follow the same pattern as pages 2 to 5. First, name each new letter and its sound. Next, ask your child to practise writing the small letter. Then, say together the name of each picture out loud. Ask your child to draw a line to link the featured letter with the pictures that begin with the same initial letter sound. Finally, complete the letters of the alphabet at the bottom of the page by filling in the missing letters.

pages 8 and 9

pages 10 and 11

Pages 12 and 13 – Odd one out and **Missing letters**

These activities provide revision exercises featuring the letters from the previous four pages. On page 12, ask your child to look at the letter in the box on the left. Say together the sound, and then name the pictures in the row. Your child should then draw a ring around the picture that doesn't begin with this letter sound. On page 13, say together the name of each picture. Encourage your child to identify the initial letter sound and then complete the word by writing down the missing initial letter.

pages 12 and 13

Pages 14, 15, 16, 17 and 18 – Letter sounds: q, r, s, t, u, v, w, x, y and z

These activities introduce the remainder of the letters of the alphabet from *q* to *z*. The exercises follow the same pattern as the previous pages. First, name each new letter and its sound. Next, ask your child to practise writing the small letter by first tracing over the dots and then copying the letter several times. For the next exercise, say together the name of each picture. Ask your child to draw a line to link the featured letter with the pictures that begin with the same initial letter sound. Page 17 features the letter *x*, which does not occur very often as an initial letter. In this exercise, your child links the letter with those pictures that have the *x* sound somewhere in the word – not just at the beginning. Finally, he or she completes the letters of the alphabet at the bottom of the page by filling in the missing letters.

Page 19 – Odd one out

This revision page features letters from the previous five pages. Ask your child to look at the letter in the box on the left. Say together the sound, and then name the pictures in that row. Your child should then ring the picture that doesn't begin with this letter sound. (Note that the letter *q* also includes *u*. Explain that *q* is never written by itself, it is always followed by *u*. One way to help your child to remember this is to say that *q* stands for queen and the *u* is a friend, who is always there to carry the crown.) Then say together the name of each picture. Ask your child to identify the initial letter sound (or the last letter sound in the case of *x*) and then complete the word by writing down the missing letter.

pages 14 and 15

pages 16 and 17

page 18

page 19

Page 27 – A story

On this page, ask your child to fill in the missing letters to complete the words in this fun story. Use the picture clues to help sound out the missing letters from the beginning, the middle or the end of the words. Read the story bit by bit with your child as he or she works through the activity. Once it is finished, read through the whole story together.

page 27

Pages 28 and 29 – Puzzle page

In each of these activities, first ask your child to write over the dotted letters and then use the picture clues to complete the words in the simple crosswords. Name the pictures to help your child work out the missing letters in each word.

pages 28 and 29

Pages 30, 31 and 32 – Play I spy

These three pages feature picture scenes that include many familiar objects beginning with specific letter sounds. Your child should find and name as many objects as possible for each of the listed letters, count them up and then write the total number in the box. Your child can also include abstract words, such as *under* or *wet*, if he or she wishes. To help with counting, either keep a tally for your child or write the initial letters lightly on the objects as they are found. These activities will be easier to tackle if your child completes the counting task before colouring the picture.

pages 30 and 31

page 32

Pages 20 and 21 – Small letters and capitals

The task is to match up the letter pairs and to practise letter recognition of both small letters and their capitals. These letter pairs don't always look the same, but they do make the same sound. Say together the sound that each letter makes, and then ask your child to draw a line between each small letter and its capital letter.

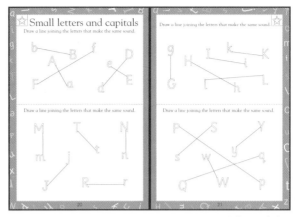

pages 20 and 21

Pages 22, 23, 24, 25 and 26 – Vowel sounds: a, e, i, o and u

These activities help children to identify vowel sounds when they occur in the middle of words. First say the vowel sound. Then name the pictures (say together each word clearly). Encourage your child to listen carefully to identify whether or not the featured vowel sound is in each word. If it is, ask your child to draw a line linking the picture to the vowel. The second exercise on each page requires your child to write the featured vowel in the middle of words. Help your child by first naming each of the pictures and then spelling out the words using their short letter sounds.

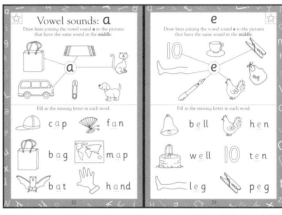

pages 22 and 23

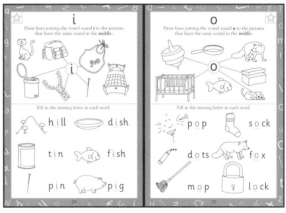

pages 24 and 25

page 26